WITHDRAWN

MAGNA CARTA

Written and illustrated by

C. WALTER HODGES

COWARD-McCANN, INC. NEW YORK

The author thanks Encyclopaedia Britannica Films Inc. for the right to reproduce the illustrations in this book.

Library of Congress Catalog Card Number: 66-12044

PRINTED IN AUSTRIA

When after the Battle of Hastings in 1066 William of Normandy
became King of England, he lost no time in sharing out the whole country
among the adventurous French and Norman knights who had helped
him to conquer it, and whose next task was to subdue it completely. This
was soon done. In every part of the land the new lords built their great
stone castles, the centres of their power, and for a hundred years they
ruled the country among themselves, more or less as they pleased. These
were the barons. They paid homage to the King for the great lands they

3

owned in his name, they paid certain taxes, and with their followers owed
military service to the King when he needed it; but there, for the most
part, their duties ended. Each in his own domain, the barons lived like
kings themselves. They had their own knights and tenants who did
homage to them as if to the king, and the peasants who tilled the fields
were bound to their lord and his lands in feudal servitude, they and their
heirs forever, or so they supposed. The baron's word was law. His justice
was harsh and often hard to find.

Here is a picture of a feudal countryside. It is an imaginary place, but
let us suppose it is somewhere in the north of England, where resistance
to the Norman overlords had been more stubborn than in the south, and
where punishment for rebellion had been severe. On the stony hill-side

in the background the great keep of the baron's castle dominates the land; the huts of the poor peasants are huddled in its shadow. All day long the peasants are working in their strips of field. The baron and his family are not here now, in this castle, for the baron has lands and castles all over England, which he visits in turn throughout the year. His bailiff and some armed men have been left in charge, with perhaps some of his most trusted knights, and these can be seen in the middle distance, beyond the gallows. And the gallows? Well, there are outlaws, there are poachers, there are always trouble-makers of one sort or another. The bodies which hang on the gallows will set an example to them. Who knows what has been happening in this case? Who cares? Only perhaps the peasant women in the foreground, and the little boy.

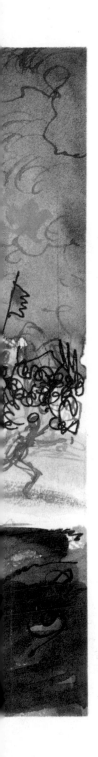

But though the baron's word was law in his own domain, it was not law for the baron next door. Quarrels over territory, and armed raids across disputed borders, were common. Villages were burnt down and castles besieged in local wars which the King himself could not prevent. King William had kept a stronger hold on things in his day, but his first successors were men less able than he, and the barons, once they had firmly established themselves, had grown greedy for more and still more power and possession. Then a time came when not only rival barons but rival claimants for the throne itself struggled for power in England. For eighteen long years the opposed armies of King Stephen and Queen Matilda fought each other up and down the land, killing and plundering and bringing wretchedness to rich and poor alike.

7

In such a land what was needed was the rule of a strong king. But where there is no law except power, and no security but by brute force, a king must be a tyrant or he cannot rule; yet if he is a tyrant his rule will be hated by all, and his kingdom will not prosper. The wise king knows that he cannot rule except by the law of the land, which must be made binding upon all people: upon the great baron in his castle, upon the knight in his manor, the peasant in his cottage, and the merchant in his

counting-house in the city. But how far should the law be binding upon
the King himself? And how far should it be binding upon the bishops of
the Church, who claimed their authority not from the King, but from
the Pope in Rome? These two great questions were soon to be put to
the test.

9

After the anarchy and tumult of the days of Stephen and Matilda, England had the good fortune to be ruled for thirty-five years by a strong king who devoted his reign and his great energies to establishing law and order throughout his vast possessions. Henry II was one of the most capable rulers of the Middle Ages. It must be remembered that since the Conquest the King of England did not rule only over England, but over Normandy and the near-by territories of Maine and Anjou as well; and Henry II by his marriage to the heiress of Aquitaine had also acquired a great area of the land of France reaching all the way to the Spanish border. It was a territory bigger than the King of France himself possessed. Over all this King Henry established a rule of law. But he came up against an unexpected difficulty. The Archbishop of Canterbury was by custom the King of England's chief minister and adviser, and King Henry had taken some trouble to see that this great office was held by his friend Thomas Becket. He had not expected that Becket would thwart him on what might appear at first sight a small matter of law. But was it so small? The question was, simply, if a priest were to commit a civil crime in England, by what court of law should he be tried? By the King's Court, said the King, since the Law of England is the King's Law. Not so, said the Archbishop, no priest owes allegiance to the King of England or to his Law. All priests belong to the Church of Rome, and must be tried by Church Law and by the Bishops whom the Pope, not the King, has appointed.

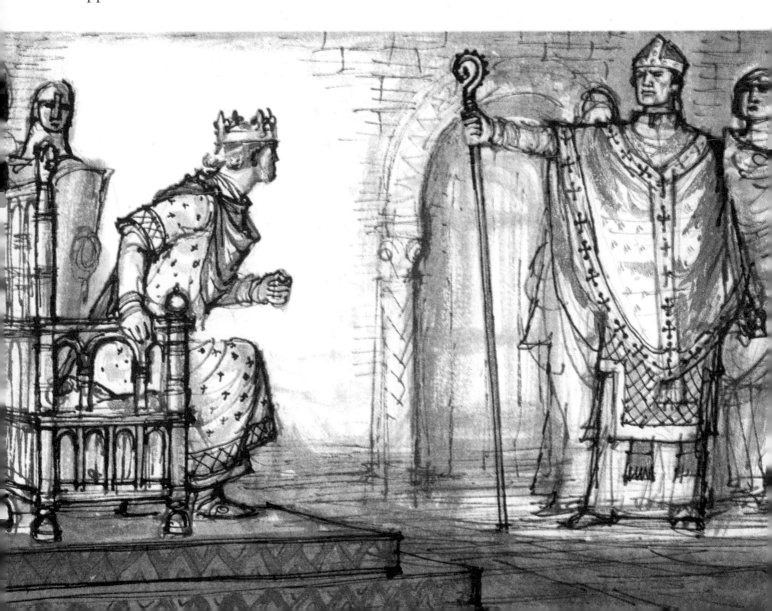

On this matter neither side would give way. The quarrel lasted for many years, until at last the King was heard to say in anger that he wished he could be rid of this hindering Archbishop. Four of his knights who heard this took him at his word. They rode to Canterbury and there slew Thomas Becket in his Cathedral. It was a deed that has never been forgotten, and forever afterwards has darkened the reputation of a great king. The point is clearly to be seen. The King must be master. He would tolerate no opposition and no authority equal to his own. If he were angry, an Archbishop might be suddenly murdered and the murderers go free. So it seemed that the law was not as binding upon the King as upon his subjects. This was tyranny. Certainly the King had worked all his reign to establish a firm and better form of law, but it was a law that still depended upon the personal and perhaps changeable wish and will of the King himself. What would happen if the next king were less personally concerned for the law than King Henry was? That in fact was what occurred.

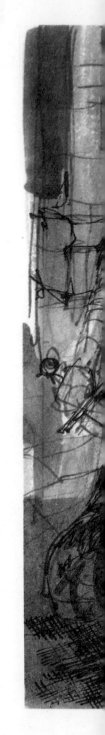

13

Henry's son Richard, when he came to the throne, had little concern in England except to raise money there, to pay for the crusades and other military adventures by which he earned himself the name of Lion Heart. He himself hardly ever visited England in all his life. He lived and died and was buried in France; and while his throne in England stood empty, the government was left in the bad hands of his brother John. On Richard's death John became King. He inherited an empty treasury and a continuous war with France, for the French King was now trying to regain those great provinces which had come to England, as if they were so much furniture and linen, in the dowry of Henry II's Queen. The English barons, however, were not very eager to fight for them, though they considered, for the dignity of the throne, that King John ought somehow to fight and keep them himself. John would have needed to be very clever to have managed this situation well. But he was not especially clever. He was cunning and he was shifty. He was also cruel. He has been described as the worst king who ever sat on the English throne, altogether unworthy and unwise. If we follow this view here it is fair to add to it that some people think he was not so black as he is often painted, no worse in fact than most of his barons, and that as a ruler in a difficult situation and a bad time he showed himself both energetic and resourceful. It was also his misfortune to be opposed by an unusually able King of France.

He very soon gave the King of France a good enough reason to declare him a criminal (which would mean that his French possessions could therefore be considered legally forfeited and should be returned to their previous overlords). John had a young nephew, Arthur, Duke of Brittany, who had claims upon some of John's provinces in France. With the help of the French King it looked, rather remotely it is true, as if he might one day be used, to make a claim even for the English throne itself. John led an expedition against this young man, captured him, and put him in prison. Arthur was never seen again. Almost certainly he was murdered by King John's orders (some say even by King John's own hand); and the King of France gained many allies as a result of it.

Distrusting his barons the King hired and relied upon mercenary troops, a private army who had to be paid on the nail, and, to get the money for this, helped the King to collect his taxes. The King rewarded his mercenary officers by giving them positions in local government. They were King's men and looked after the King's interests (next only to their own) without regard to the welfare of the land or the people.

The King's officers now confronted the barons, one by one, with a burden of taxation unlike anything they had known before. There was a customary payment, known as 'scutage', which a knight or his lord had to pay in place of giving direct military service to the King. There were many barons who did not wish to send their knights to serve with the King's army. The King now greatly increased the scutage. He also levied heavy fines on barons who did not themselves join him on his campaigns. He infringed and offended against the customary rights of the barons in every way, and as things grew worse and the barons angrier he took hostages from them to ensure their good behaviour. This, as the barons rightly understood, meant that there was no trust in any contract of law on either side.

The hands of the King's tax-gatherers also fell heavily upon the great merchants in the cities. The collective power of the burgesses of great cities such as London and Norwich, with their wealthy trade guilds, markets and exchanges, was now for the first time beginning to make itself felt. It was unwise, to say the least, to anger both barons and citizens at the same time. It was still more unwise to top this off by angering the Church as well.

Once again, as in King Henry's time, the trouble was over Canterbury.
A new Archbishop was to be elected, and there were two candidates: the
King favoured one of them, the monks of Canterbury the other. The
Pope insisted that the election must take place before him personally, to
see fair play. He then discovered that King John was trying to cheat him;

the monks of Canterbury confessed
that the King had somehow per-
suaded them to vote for his candidate,

not for theirs. Thereupon the Pope presented a candidate of his own, a wise and scholarly Englishman named Stephen Langton, who had been for many years the Pope's friend. The monks elected Langton, who then came before the King for acceptance.

King John was furious. He refused to accept Langton as Archbishop. He banished the monks of Canterbury. He seized Church property and threatened that in future he would refuse to allow English priests to appeal to the court of Rome in any such matters.

The Pope replied by placing the whole country under an Interdict. This meant that the sacraments and consolations of the Church were forbidden to all people in King John's dominions. The churches were closed. No one might be buried, married, baptized, or forgiven their sins, and all because of King John.

So the King found himself faced with a rebellious barony, a disgruntled citizenry, a hostile Church, and a whole people put to misery because of his tyranny and mismanagement. And while John was occupied in trying to patch over the cracks of his bad government in England, trying to find money, trying to find soldiers willing to serve him, the King of France and his nobles were invading and cutting away piece by piece his dominions across the Channel. The great new territories his father had acquired had always been loosely held and so in some danger of being lost; but it was not these that went first. The first to be lost were Normandy, Maine, and Anjou, the traditional homelands of King John's ancestors, which were to him more like his own country than England itself. He became scornfully known as 'John Lack-Land'.

Now all classes of people could clearly see that no one could be free or safe unless the laws of the land were good and just, and unless they were as binding upon the King as upon themselves. The King could not be allowed to put himself above the law; security could not be allowed to depend on the mere chance of one man's will, which might be benevolent at one moment and hostile the next, liable to change from day to day or from king to king. The limit's of the King's power must be clearly laid down.

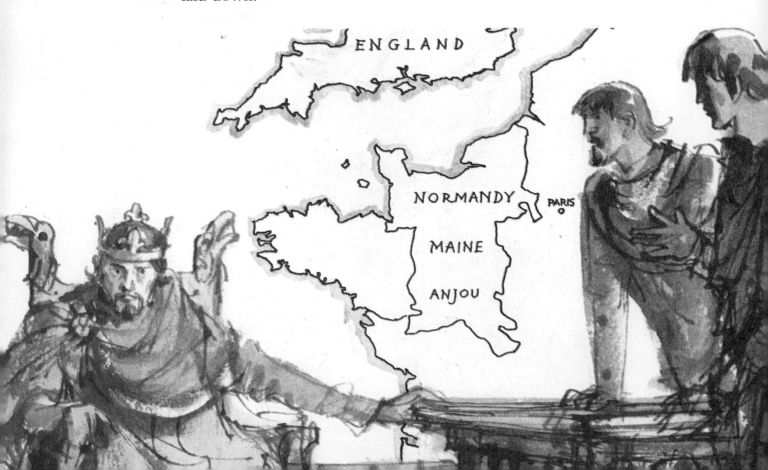

King John, meanwhile, was trying to wriggle out of his difficulties as best he could without giving too much away. He decided it would serve his turn better to make peace with the Church than with the barons, so he at last accepted Stephen Langton as Archbishop of Canterbury; and the Pope then absolved John and his country from the Interdict. So far so good. But now, as soon as he had been consecrated and installed at Canterbury, Archbishop Stephen Langton took a hand. It was clear to him, as to all responsible men, that there ought to be a form of written contract between the King and his subjects, laying down the rights and liberties of all in a way which no one thereafter could deny or turn a blind eye upon.

In fact there was one old contract of this kind already in existence, dating from the days of King John's grandfather, Henry I; but it had never received any attention. Stephen Langton now studied it, worked upon it, enlarged and strengthened it, and so created a new document which he presented for approval before a great assembly of people, including many powerful barons, justices and leading citizens, at St. Paul's in London. This was the beginning of Magna Carta—the Great Charter.

The King had no time to take much notice of this. He was in a rage with the barons of the North Country, who had failed to join his army for an expedition to France. He would have marched against them, but Stephen Langton managed to dissuade him. When at last he did succeed in raising enough troops for the French campaign, it all turned out a disaster. Back in England the King demanded scutage from the barons, to pay for it, and the barons refused. They gathered in a great assembly at Bury St. Edmunds, and there King John went to meet them. There, too, was Stephen Langton with the Charter. The meeting ended without agreement, but after the King had gone the barons solemnly vowed that all would withdraw their allegiance from him unless he would put his hand to the Charter and so confirm their liberties.

The meeting at Bury St. Edmunds took place in November 1214. Negotiations between the barons and the King then went on all through the winter and the following spring. Each side hoped to wear the other down. Neither would give way. Back and forth between them went the patiently working Archbishop. John may have been hoping he could win the support of the citizens and merchant classes against the barons, and he was playing for time. Then, in May 1215, the barons lost what was left of their patience, renounced their allegiance, and stood in open rebellion against the King. They chose for their leader the baron Robert FitzWalter, who took the title of 'Marshall of the Army of God and Holy Church'.

John now played his last card and appealed to the cities. But the merchants had not forgotten his previous rough handling and taxing of them. London led the way and declared in favour of the barons. Faced at last with a confederacy of Church, barons, and merchant citizens, King John knew that he would have to come to terms. He called a truce.

The King with his forces was at Windsor. The army of the barons was five miles away at Staines. Midway between the two, in the River Thames, was a little island meadow called Runnymede. Here on this neutral ground and in sight of their two armies the King and the barons met, and for six days bargained upon the document which ever since has been regarded as the foundation Charter of the liberties of the English-speaking peoples. One can imagine the scene as if it were some great international conference in our own time: the leading figures of both sides, the King, the Archbishop, Robert FitzWalter, and the rest arriving each day at the island; and, in the meadows on either side of the river, the tents for all the lawyers, clerks and advisers who were expected to work out details and keep the records of the debates; then the cook-houses and dining-tents, the tented chapel, the horse-lines, and the guest-tent for visitors. There would be no end of coming and going between the two camps and this conference place on the little island where the standard of England flapped on its tall pole, showing that the King was there.

Wherever one looks closely into history one finds that what had at first seemed a simple story is never really quite so simple, that the bad man is seldom quite so obviously bad, nor the good man so absolutely good as the simplified story would have us believe. It is so in this case, and our story has perhaps been too simply told all along. But the Great Charter itself is a complicated document, often dealing with things and situations long gone by, and it may be hard to say why this document and not any other—the old Charter of Henry I, for example—is now rightly regarded as the fixing-point of our liberties. But so, quite simply, it is. Here in the water-meadow, in June 1215, a tyrant king met with a gang of barons half of whom perhaps, in his shoes, would have been every inch as bad as he, all on each side being out to get as much personal power as they could, for better or worse; and yet between them all they laid down in detail the rights of individual liberty, the rights of property, and the ways to the right administration of the law. ('. . . *No free man shall be taken, imprisoned, disseised of his freehold or liberties or free customs, or be outlawed or exiled or otherwise damaged, nor will we proceed against him or prosecute him, except by the lawful judgement of his peers and by the law of the land . . . To no one will we sell, to no one will we deny right or justice.*')

The truce was due to expire on June 15th, and on that day the King at last assented to the terms of the Great Charter. The picture shows the royal seal being affixed. The ribbons hanging from the parchment are placed through the open seal-mould, the hot wax is poured in, and the mould closed over it all. When the seal is taken out it will hang like a great medal impressed on both sides. The King is shown ceremonially placing his hand upon the mould, in token that this is his act and deed.

When this had been done, the Charter was taken and copied many times, and copies were sent out all over the country, to every cathedral and important city and stronghold of power. Of these many copies four are still in existence.

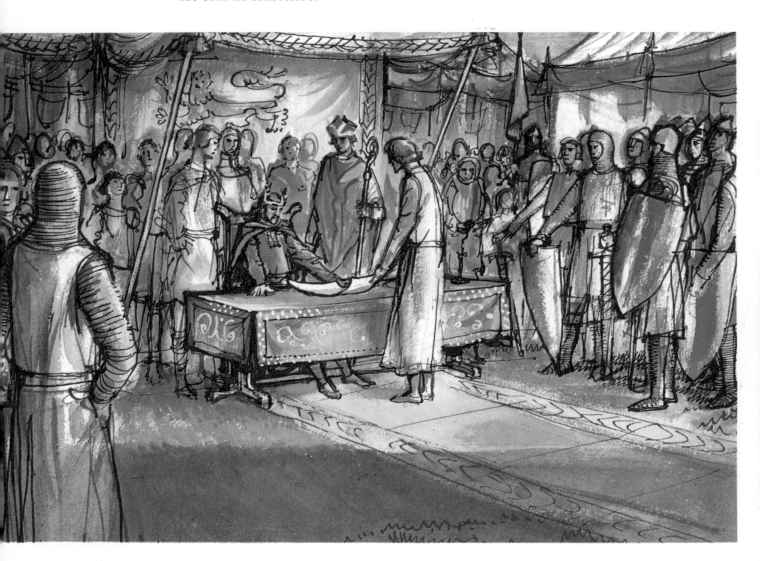

So, the King having at last assented, or having at least seemed to do so, the barons restored their allegiance to him, all once more formally doing homage. *'Let it be known that a firm peace has been made, by the Grace of God, between us and our barons, on Friday after the Feast of the Holy Trinity, at Runnymede near Staines; on which account we received their homage on that day and at that place.'*

Unfortunately, the peace did not last long. Within a few short weeks the King and the barons were again in arms, each side accusing the other of bad faith, and it looked as if the bad old days of Stephen and Matilda were to be repeated, laying the whole country under clouds of ruin and civil war. The barons had now submitted their variable allegiance to the Dauphin of France, who landed a force on the south coast. The story of King John's desperate campaign, his rapid marches with his army of mercenaries from one end of the country to the other, makes reading worthy of a better cause. Then in the autumn of the next year, hurrying against time, and taking a risky short-cut across the sands of the Lincolnshire Wash, he was caught by the unexpectedly rapid flowing-in of the tide. He himself escaped; but all his long baggage-train, the heavy loaded carts and sumpter-horses of an army three thousand strong, were caught and drowned in the treacherous sands and the rising waters. A few days later, sick and exhausted and in despair, defeated by the results of his bad character, bad judgement and bad luck, King John died. If history allowed it (which it does not), one might feel sorry for him; but instead one is obliged to say that it was fortunate for the country that he died when he did.

In the following reign of Henry III the Great Charter was confirmed and reissued. But there was still much trouble in store before it could be made properly effective. Once again the barons went to war, this time at odds with each other. It was not until after the battle at Lewes, in Sussex, in the year 1264, that a real change occurred. The winning army was led by the baron Simon de Montfort who had earned the support of that newly influential class, the merchant citizens, guildsmen and burgesses, the 'commons'. The victorious de Montfort summoned a great Parliament at Westminster, and to this assembly there came not only the great feudal lords, but also, for the first time, ordinary knights from the country shires, and 'borough members' representing the merchant classes from the towns. This was a small beginning which later was to grow into the modern House of Commons.

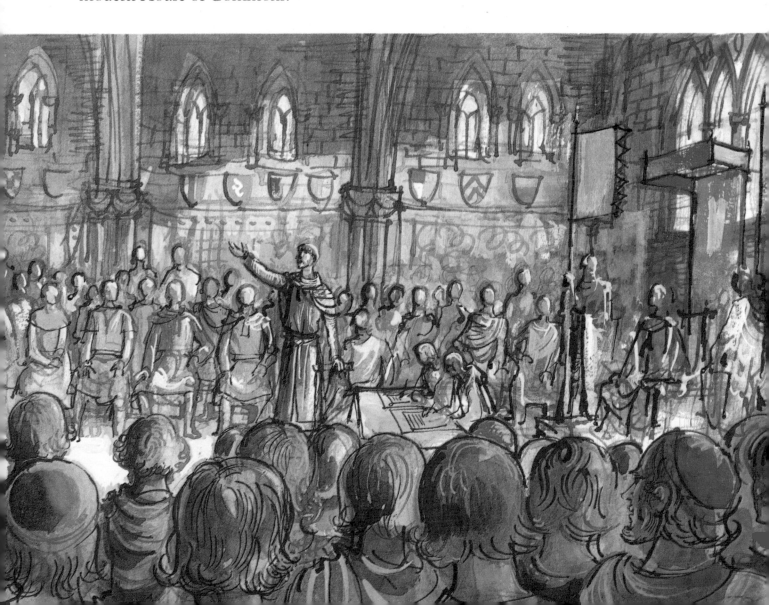

It was the Great Charter which first established the supremacy of the law of the land over the will and power of the King. It assumed, as the Lord Chancellor of England said when speaking on the anniversary of Magna Carta in 1965, 'that the government shall be a government of laws, and not of men'. And in the end it was Parliament, broadly representing all classes of people in town and country, which came to make and watch over those laws.